Elie Wiesel

A Holocaust Survivor Cries Out for Peace

by Sarah Houghton

Reading Consultant:
Timothy Rasinski, Ph.D.
Professor of Reading Education
Kent State University

Content Consultant:
John K. Roth, Ph.D.
Edward J. Sexton Professor of
Philosophy and Director, Center
for the Study of the Holocaust,
Genocide, and Human Rights
Claremont McKenna College

Red Brick™ Learning

Published by Red Brick™ Learning
7825 Telegraph Road, Bloomington, Minnesota 55438
http://www.redbricklearning.com

Library of Congress Cataloging-in-Publication Data
Houghton, Sarah, 1978–
    Elie Wiesel: a Holocaust survivor cries out for peace / by Sarah Houghton.
    p. cm.—(High five reading)
    Summary: A biography of author, speaker, and Nobel Peace Prize winner
Elie Wiesel, focusing on his childhood in a Nazi concentration camp and
his efforts to ensure that there will never be another Holocaust.
Includes bibliographical references and index.
    ISBN 0-7368-2792-7 (hc)—ISBN 0-7368-2833-8 (pbk.)
    1.Wiesel, Elie, 1928—Juvenile literature. 2. Jews—Romania—Sighet—
Biography—Juvenile literature. 3. Holocaust, Jewish (1939-1945)—Romania—
Sighet—Juvenile literature. 4. Holocaust survivors—Biography—Juvenile
literature. [1. Wiesel, Elie, 1928– 2. Authors, French. 3. Holocaust survivors.
4. Holocaust, Jewish (1939-1945) 5. Jews—Biography. 6. Nobel Prizes—
Biography.] I. Title. II. Series.
DS135.R73W544 2003
940.53'18'092—dc21

                            2003009762

Created by Kent Publishing Services, Inc.
Executive Editor: Robbie Butler
Designed by Signature Design Group, Inc.
This publisher has made every effort to trace ownership of all copyrighted
material and to secure necessary permissions. In the event of any questions
arising as to the use of any material, the publisher, while expressing regret for
any inadvertent error, will be happy to make necessary corrections.

Photo Credits:
Cover, pages 4, 10, 13, 15, 27, Hulton-Deutsch Collection/Corbis; pages 8, 28,
United States Holocaust Memorial Museum; page 11, 20, 23, 30, 33,
Bettmann/Corbis; page 16, David G. Houser/Corbis; pages 7, 19, 34, Ira
Nowinski/Corbis; pages 37, 40, Sygma/Corbis; page 39, Owen Franken/Corbis;
page 43, James P. Blair/Corbis

Printed in the United States of America.
1 2 3 4 5 6 08 07 06 05 04 03

Table of Contents

CHAPTER 1

Dangerous Times

Think of a time when something really bad happened to you. Can you remember it well? Does the memory make you different? Does it change the way you live now?

Death on the Train

It is 1945. A train rattles through Germany in the dark night. The air is as cold as ice. Snow is falling. The train cars have no roofs. Snowflakes fall on the forms inside. The snow is silent, but the train is filled with the sound of moaning.

The train cars are cattle wagons. But the wagons carry no cattle. They carry men who are tightly packed together. Some of the men have died. But there is no room for anyone to lie down. In the freezing weather, it is not easy to tell the living from the dead.

moaning: a long, low sound of sorrow or pain
cattle wagon: a train car used to carry cows

Fighting for Food

Suddenly, there is a shout. The train screeches to a halt. The men hear German voices. The Germans throw something to them. The men grab at it. It's bread. But it's hard and old. And there is not much of it.

The men in the wagons are starving. They have had nothing to eat for days, except snow. They begin to struggle for the bread. Brothers, fathers, and sons fight one another for it. Hunger is making them crazy. The German men outside laugh at the starving people fighting for food, for life.

---

screech: to give a harsh, high sound

In one wagon, a boy sees the fighting but does not join the battle for bread. The boy is starving, just like the others, but he struggles to help his sick father. They have been close to death many times in the last months. The boy will not let his father give up on life now.

The train shudders into motion again. The men have no idea where the train is going. No one knows if they will live to find out, and certainly not the boy, whose name is Elie Wiesel (EL-ee wee-ZEL).

Freight cars like these were used to transport Jews and other prisoners to concentration camps.

shudder: to shake or tremble

A Faithful Jewish Family

Elie Wiesel was born in 1928. His parents, Shlomo (SHLOH-moh) and Sarah, lived in a village called Sighet (SEE-get). Today, Sighet is in Romania, a country in Europe.

Elie's parents were Jewish. They raised Elie and his three sisters to live by the teachings of the Jewish faith. Elie loved to learn about Judaism.

Elie Wiesel grew up in the village of Sighet.

---

faith: a particular religion
Judaism: the religion of the Jewish people

Troubles Grow

As Elie grew up, his world became more dangerous. Adolf Hitler and the Nazi Party took control of Germany in 1933. Hitler wanted to take over all of Europe, including Elie's country.

In 1939, World War II (1939–1945) broke out in Europe. During this war, the Nazis and their followers murdered millions of Jews and other people. The Nazis had planned to kill all Jews in German-controlled countries. The Nazi destruction of Jewish life came to be called the Holocaust.

Holocaust: the killing of millions of European Jews and others by the Nazis during World War II

— CHAPTER **2** —

The Holocaust

Imagine soldiers breaking into your home. They force you and your family to board a train to a prison camp. Imagine watching soldiers drag your parents, brothers, or sisters away. Imagine knowing that your family will die in that camp.

Nazi supporters salute Adolf Hitler.

Spreading Hate

Adolf Hitler wanted the Nazis to rule Germany—and all of Europe.

Hitler believed that Germans were better than other people. He believed that people from other countries, cultures, and religions were inferior to Germans. He also felt this way about people with disabilities. He wanted the German people to look down on anyone who was not like them. Hitler was good at making people believe in his ideas.

Most of all, Hitler hated the Jews. Hitler and the Nazi Party planned to kill all the Jews in Europe. This plan was called the "Final Solution."

Adolf Hitler

---

culture: the way of life of a certain group of people
inferior: not as good as someone else
solution: the answer to a problem

The Night of Broken Glass

A major attack on the Jewish people happened the night of November 9, 1938. Nazi leaders ordered Jewish property in Germany to be destroyed. Jewish stores were smashed and homes were looted. Many synagogues were set on fire.

This attack by the Germans became known as Kristallnacht (KRIS-tul-nokt). This means "Night of Broken Glass." The name comes from the millions of windows broken on Jewish property throughout Germany during that awful night.

loot: to rob or take by force
synagogue: a building where Jews worship and study

A man shovels broken glass from a Jewish storefront. The night before, known as Kristallnacht, German mobs murdered Jewish people and destroyed their property.

Jewish Life Destroyed

The Nazis and their followers did more than break windows on Kristallnacht. They desecrated Jewish cemeteries. German mobs attacked Jews, killing at least 90 of them. About 30,000 Jewish men were taken from their families, locked up, and cruelly treated. Some were murdered.

But Kristallnacht was just the start. In the next weeks, the German government passed new laws. These laws took away Jewish property. They stopped Jews from getting jobs. Businesses belonging to Jews were closed. Jewish children were not allowed to go to school. Jews could not go to movies or concerts. Even their driver's licenses were taken away.

---

desecrate: to destroy or damage something sacred
cemetery: a place where dead bodies are buried

Two Nazis post a sign that says,
"Germans!
Defend yourselves.
Do not buy from Jews!"

Death Camps

Nazi Germany was getting rid of its Jews. The Nazis took the Jews and other groups of people they did not like to prisons called concentration camps. One of the worst camps was Auschwitz (OWSH-vitz). The Nazis set up this camp in 1940. It was in Poland, a country occupied by the Germans.

Prisoners were held in these buildings at Auschwitz.

concentration camp: a prison for people thought to be dangerous to the ruling group
occupy: to take control of a place by capturing it

In 1942, Auschwitz became more than a concentration camp. It became a death camp. A part of Auschwitz, called Birkenau (BIRK-eh-now), became the Holocaust's major site of mass murder.

Most of the Jewish men, women, and children taken to Auschwitz were put to death in gas chambers as soon as they arrived. The Nazis made the gas chambers to look like shower rooms. But instead of water, poison gas poured out. Anyone in those rooms was dead in a few minutes.

The gas chambers at Auschwitz-Birkenau were essential for Nazi Germany's "Final Solution." Today, all over the world, Auschwitz is a symbol of the horror of the Holocaust. About 6 million Jews were among the many millions of people who were murdered by Hitler's followers.

---

chamber: a room or group of connected rooms
essential: most important
symbol: something that represents another thing or idea

Living in Fear

In March 1944, Elie was a teenager. But he was not allowed to live like most teenagers today. Like other Jews in Europe, he suffered under the laws of the Nazis. Even so, Elie's friends and neighbors did not believe the death camps existed. They thought they were stories made up to frighten the Jews.

One spring day in 1944, Elie was taken away with his father, mother, and sisters. They were crammed into a train car. Soon, the people in these trains would know the Nazi camps were real. Elie's family and thousands of others were being deported to Auschwitz.

What will happen to the Wiesels?

What will happen to Elie?

---

deport: to force to leave a country

The gateway arch at Auschwitz displays the camp's motto—"work makes one free."

CHAPTER 3

Horror without End

Elie's old life was gone. Many people died on the way to the death camps. Elie and his family did not. But how long could they endure the horror of the camps?

Concentration camp prisoners in their barracks. Elie Wiesel is on the second bunk from the bottom, seventh from the left.

Work or Die

Elie and his family arrived at Auschwitz in May 1944. The guards first separated the men and women. What happened next depended on how healthy you looked. Only those who looked fit to work were saved from death. The prison guards sent Elie's mother and little sister straight to the gas chambers. The Germans had no use for them, so they were murdered.

Elie and his father were fit enough to work. This meant that they would work as slave laborers. Their labor camp was in another part of Auschwitz called Buna (BOO-nah) or Monowitz (MAH-no-witz).

---

slave laborer: a worker who is forced to work for no wages

Forced to Watch Death

Conditions in the camps were horrible. There was very little food. Elie and the other prisoners got just a little bread and soup. Many people starved to death.

Sometimes the Nazis hanged people in front of the other prisoners. Everyone, even young people like Elie, had to watch.

Guards beat people for the smallest reasons. Once, Elie was whipped in public. He got 25 brutal lashes. Every day Elie had to struggle against despair. Elie and his father spent eight months as slave workers in Buna.

---

condition: the way something is
despair: the condition of giving up hope

Hiding the Evidence

By 1945, Germany was losing World War II. Germany's enemies, the Allies, were getting closer to the death camps. Those in charge of the camps knew the Allies would learn what they had done.

So the Germans tried to hide the evidence. At Auschwitz, the gas chambers were knocked down. Most of the remaining prisoners were moved. Would the Germans get away with their crimes?

Dead bodies of concentration camp prisoners

evidence: something that shows or proves something
Allies: the nations that fought against Germany and its partners in World War II

Death March

The Allies moved closer to Auschwitz. The Germans had to get away fast.

The Germans sent some of the prisoners deeper into German territory. Elie, his father, and many others were marched to Gleiwitz (GLYE-vitz), Poland. They had to cover 42 miles (68 kilometers) without food or rest. Guards shot anyone who fell behind.

Map of Germany and Poland, 1944

---

territory: the land ruled by a nation

At Gleiwitz, Elie and his father were crammed into open train cars. The men were starving. Sometimes, people outside threw old bread to the prisoners. They liked to watch them fight for the food.

The trains took the prisoners to another concentration camp, in Buchenwald (BOO-kin-vawld), Germany. They joined other prisoners already there. Not long after the Wiesels arrived, Elie's father died.

On April 11, as American troops approached, the Buchenwald guards fled, and the prisoners liberated the camp.

---

liberate: to set free

Liberation?

The American troops who arrived at Buchenwald were sickened by what they saw. They found piles of dead bodies. They saw signs of torture and cremation. The Germans had failed to hide the horror of their actions.

The starving prisoners looked like skeletons. Their skin was stretched over their bones. All of the prisoners were scarred. Some scars were physical. Some were emotional. It was impossible to say which were worse.

Buchenwald wasn't the only proof of the Holocaust. Russian Allied troops liberated a Nazi concentration camp in July 1944. This was the first camp to be set free. Allied troops found other death camps as well. All gave proof of Nazi war crimes to the world.

---

torture: the act of causing great pain in order to force someone to do something against his or her will
cremation: the burning of dead bodies
scar: to have an effect on the mind or body
emotional: having to do with feelings and thought

Free, but Alone

Elie was free. But it was a lonely freedom. His father, mother, and little sister had died in the camps. He did not know where his other sisters were. Where could he go?

Prisoners of the Dachau concentration camp celebrate their liberation from behind a barbed wire fence on May 3, 1945. Dachau and other death camps gave proof of Nazi war crimes to the world.

— CHAPTER **4** —

Another Journey

As we begin this chapter, Elie again is going to Auschwitz. Only this time, it is July 1979, and Elie is a free man. Why is he going back to Auschwitz? To understand, we must look at what happened to Elie after the war.

Jewish children pose for a photo in a children's home in France. Elie lived in such a home after the war.

Coming Back to Life

Back in 1945, when Elie was freed, a French charity took care of him. It also sent him to school. But Elie struggled to lead his new, free life. He felt alone and deeply sad. Many others who survived the Holocaust felt the same way.

But Elie did not give in to these feelings. After studying in Paris, he became a journalist. In 1958, he wrote a book about the Holocaust, called *Night*. People all over the world read *Night*. The book told of the horror and evil of the Holocaust. Elie would write many other books as well. In 1963, he became a U.S. citizen. Elie later became a teacher. He also became known as an expert on the Holocaust.

charity: an organization that cares for needy people
journalist: a person who writes about the news
expert: a person who has special knowledge and experience

Deciding How to Remember

In 1978, U.S. President Jimmy Carter set up the President's Commission on the Holocaust. The Commission included people from many different backgrounds. It included people of different faiths, survivors of the Holocaust, and scholars.

Jimmy Carter stands with Elie Wiesel, chairperson of the President's Commission on the Holocaust.

---

commission: a group of people chosen to do something
survivor: a person who continues to live despite hardship
scholar: a person who has learned much through study

The Commission wanted to find out the best ways to remember the Holocaust. It also wanted to find the best ways to share the lessons that the Holocaust might teach. Elie was chosen to be the committee chairperson.

In 1979, Elie and other members of the Commission set off on a fact-finding mission. They traveled to several countries to learn what others were doing to remember the Holocaust. They visited memorials and museums. They went to the places where millions of Jews had been killed. They studied the many ways people remembered the Holocaust and honored those killed.

---

chairperson: the person in charge
fact-finding mission: a trip taken to find information
memorial: anything meant to remind people of an event or person

Going Back to Face Evil

The Commission went to Auschwitz.
Elie went back to the places where the
Nazis had kept him prisoner, and where
they had murdered his mother and sister.
He remembered that horrible time,
years before.

This time, though, Elie wasn't starving.
This time, he was no longer a boy. It was
very hard for Elie and the other Auschwitz
survivors to walk back into the camp.
It took great courage.

Elie had to face again the places where he
had seen people murdered. He saw the gas
chambers where his mother and sister had
died. Some members of the Commission
said prayers. Some sang songs of memory.
But no words could show how they felt.

Back Home in America

Elie and the group returned to the United States. He wrote and spoke about what he had learned. Elie reminded Americans to question what their leaders do. He warned about leaders who try to take too much power, the way Hitler did.

Elie also worked with others to help create the United States Holocaust Memorial Museum in Washington, D.C. If you visit the museum, you will see why Elie believes the Holocaust is something we must never forget.

Elie Wiesel mixes soil from the Nazi concentration camp of Auschwitz with ground under the U.S. Holocaust Memorial Museum building.

CHAPTER 5

Working for Peace

Elie rebuilt his life. He became a successful writer and teacher. He shared his terrible past. He showed America how to remember the horror. But he has a greater message to share. What do you think his message is?

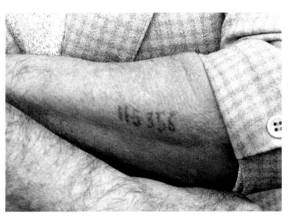

The Nazis even tried to take people's names. In the camps, people were marked with numbers. Elie's number was A-7713.

Speaking for the Silent

Elie believes that all people have the right to live without fear of hunger or persecution. Governments should not put in prison or kill people who criticize their actions. If people don't speak out, other mass killings will happen. Some already have.

Elie helps those who are persecuted because of their religion or color. He speaks out for minorities, refugees, and victims of hunger and war.

Elie questions those in power and asks why past mistakes happened. He hopes to prevent the same mistakes from happening again.

Elie has asked U.S. presidents why no one stopped the Holocaust. He does not always get answers to his questions. But he keeps asking.

---

persecution: the condition of being treated in a cruel or harsh way
criticize: to disagree with and speak out
minority: a smaller group different from most others
refugee: a person who flees his or her country

Elie Is Criticized

Some people have criticized Elie. Some say he uses the terrible events of the death camps to make money from his books and his teaching.

But he continues his work. Elie continues to speak out. He continues to make people remember the horrors that can happen.

The Greatest Honor of All

Elie has been honored many times for his work for human rights. The quiet boy from Sighet is respected all over the world. In 1986, Elie was awarded his greatest honor of all—the Nobel Peace Prize.

---

respect: to think highly of

*Elie Wiesel has received many awards for his
human rights work. They include:*

The Nobel Peace Prize
Presidential Medal of Freedom
U.S. Congressional Gold Medal
Medal of Liberty
Award Rank of Grand-Croix
in the French Legion of Honor

The Nobel Prize

Nobel Prizes are awarded each year. They are given to persons "whose work has been of the greatest benefit to mankind." The Nobel Prize for Peace is the most famous of these prizes.

Those who chose Elie for the award called him "a messenger to mankind." They said, "his message is one of peace." They praised Elie's care for all people of all cultures.

Accepting the Award

When Elie accepted the award, he gave a speech. In the speech he talked about memory. He said how important it is to remember bad things as well as good. "It is memory that will save humanity," Elie said. His point is that only by remembering can people avoid making the same mistakes again.

---

benefit: a help or advantage
messenger: someone who speaks for others

Elie Wiesel accepts his Nobel Peace Prize.
You can read Elie's speech by going to:
http://www.historyplace.com/speeches/wiesel.htm

The Elie Wiesel Foundation

Part of the Nobel Prize for Peace is money. Elie and his wife, Marion, used the money Elie received to do something very special. They set up an organization to "advance the cause of human rights." This group brings together people from all over the world to talk, to listen, and to share ideas.

Elie and his wife, Marion

organization: a group of people who work toward the same goal
advance: to help promote

Elie's group also teaches people about the Holocaust. It helps those being persecuted today. It reminds people to never trust anyone who tells them to hate or fear certain groups of people. If we can learn this, Elie says, we will build a better world. "The memory of evil will serve as a shield against evil," he says.

Elie's group wants to help make the world a better place. Its name? The Elie Wiesel Foundation for Humanity.

The Elie Wiesel Foundation for Humanity Mission Statement

To advance the cause of human rights by creating forums for the discussion and resolution of urgent ethical issues.

Through all its activities, the Foundation seeks to combat indifference, intolerance, and injustice.

Epilogue

Remember Not To Forget

Elie Wiesel has seen evil. He has seen what hatred can do to people. He believes we should remember this hatred and these evil acts. He believes there is hope for a better future. Here are some of the things Elie said in his Nobel Prize speech:

- "For me, hope without memory is like memory without hope."

- "Just as man cannot live without dreams, he cannot live without hope."

Elie also quoted from the Talmud, which contains Jewish teachings. The Talmud says, *Talmidei hakhamim shemarbin shalom baolam.* That means, "It is the wise men who will bring about peace." Why is this? "Perhaps," says Elie, "because wise men remember best."

What do you think?

Talmud: a collection of writings that contain Jewish teachings

The United States Holocaust Memorial Museum

Teaching about the Holocaust

The U.S. Holocaust Memorial Museum opened in 1993. The museum contains exhibits about the Holocaust. The museum would like visitors to learn and think about what happened during the Holocaust. Then it would like them to think about their own actions in today's world.

---

exhibit: something that is shown or displayed to the public

Glossary

advance: to help promote

Allies: the nations that fought against Germany and its partners in World War II

benefit: a help or advantage

cattle wagon: a train car used to carry cows

cemetery: a place where dead bodies are buried

chairperson: the person in charge

chamber: a room or group of connected rooms

charity: an organization that cares for needy people

commission: a group of people chosen to do something

concentration camp: a prison for people thought to be dangerous to the ruling group

condition: the way something is

cremation: the burning of dead bodies

criticize: to disagree with and speak out

culture: the way of life of a certain group of people

deport: to force to leave a country

desecrate: to destroy or damage something sacred

despair: the condition of giving up hope

emotional: having to do with feelings and thought

essential: most important

evidence: something that shows or proves something

exhibit: something that is shown or displayed to the public

expert: a person who has special knowledge and experience

fact-finding mission: a trip taken to find information

faith: a particular religion

Holocaust: the killing of millions of European Jews and others by the Nazis during World War II

inferior: not as good as someone else

journalist: a person who writes about the news

Judaism: the religion of the Jewish people

liberate: to set free

loot: to rob or take by force

memorial: anything meant to remind people of an event or person

messenger: someone who speaks for others

minority: a smaller group different from most others

moaning: a long, low sound of sorrow or pain

occupy: to take control of a place by capturing it

organization: a group of people who work toward the same goal

persecution: the condition of being treated in a cruel or harsh way

refugee: a person who flees his or her country

respect: to think highly of

scar: to have an effect on the mind or body

scholar: a person who has learned much through study

screech: to give a harsh, high sound

shudder: to shake or tremble

slave laborer: a worker who is forced to work for no wages

solution: the answer to a problem

survivor: a person who continues to live despite hardship

symbol: something that represents another thing or idea

synagogue: a building where Jews worship and study

Talmud: a collection of writings that contain Jewish teachings

territory: the land ruled by a nation

torture: the act of causing great pain in order to force someone to do something against his or her will

Bibliography

George, Charles. *The Holocaust.* History of the World. San Diego, Calif.: Kidhaven Press, 2003.

Lawton, Clive. *Auschwitz.* Cambridge, Mass.: Candlewick Press, 2002.

Levy, Patricia. *Survival and Resistance.* Holocaust. Austin, Texas: Raintree Steck-Vaughn, 2001.

Pariser, Michael. *Elie Wiesel: Bearing Witness.* Gateway Biography. Brookfield, Conn.: Millbrook Press, 1994.

Sheehan, Sean. *After the Holocaust.* Holocaust. Austin, Texas: Raintree Steck-Vaughn, 2001.

Useful Addresses

United States Holocaust Memorial Museum
100 Raoul Wallenberg Place, SW
Washington, DC 20024-2126

The Auschwitz-Birkenau Memorial and Museum
32-620 Oswiecim
Poland

The Center for Holocaust and Genocide Studies
University of Minnesota
100 Nolte Hall West
315 Pillsbury Drive
Minneapolis, MN 55455
http://www.chgs.umn.edu

Internet Sites

The Elie Wiesel Foundation for Humanity
http://www.eliewieselfoundation.org

The History Place™ Great Speeches Collection
http://www.historyplace.com/speeches/wiesel.htm

Museum of Tolerance Online Multimedia Learning Center
http://motlc.wiesenthal.com/

United States Holocaust Memorial Museum
http://www.ushmm.org

Index